PICTURE

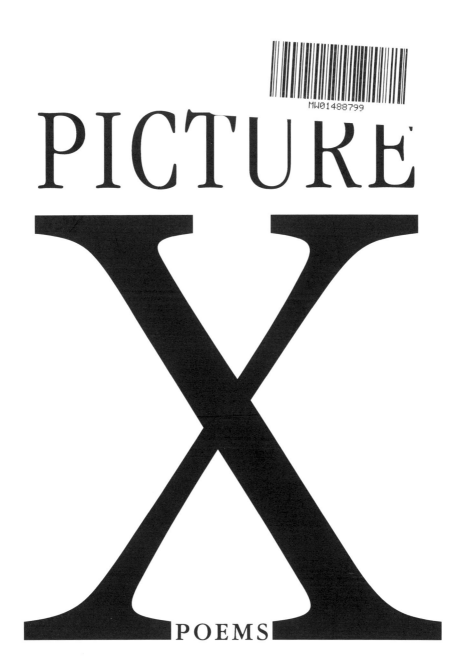

X

POEMS

TIM SHANER

Airlie Press is supported by book sales and subscription orders,
by contributions to the press from its supporters,
and by the work donated by all the poet-editors of the press.

Major funding has been provided by Julia Wills.

DESIGN: Cheryl McLean
AUTHOR PHOTO: Nora Shaner

Airlie Press
PO Box 434
Monmouth, OR 97361
editors@airliepress.org
www.airliepress.org

ISBN: 978-0-9895799-0-2
Library of Congress Control Number: 2014940563

Printed in the United States of America
Printed by Thomson-Shore on 30% postconsumer recycled paper
Processed chlorine-free

Contents

For Tammy & Nora

Nature Walks

"No Mountain bikes please. Please respect plants and wildlife.
Leaves of three (poison oak), let them be. Leave no trace,
please pack out your trash. Invasive weeds are everywhere—
please clean your boots and gear before you hike."

—spencerbutte.com

"Your Mountain needs you."

—Campaign slogan from the Eugene
Parks and Recreation Department (1976)

A Note on the Pictures

"What kind of times are they when a talk of trees is almost a crime because it implies silence about so many horrors?"

—Bertolt Brecht

Since moving out West, I had been struggling with my desire to write out West—the action of writing itself being the point, or *point enough*—out West or not—and with the frustration of not knowing how to write in such a setting as this one with the nature all around naturally out West. Having to deal with the beauty out West, not construct it as we liked to think we did back East in Buffalo, New York. Though beauty was hardly in mind in the City of No Illusions. How to write in this place, yet finding myself writing nonetheless out West, yet dissatisfied with the words out West, still being *used*, as if windows, as if it was natural, like some kind of default mode, and that in being employed as such I was looking right past the words, even the windows, for that matter, dazzled as I was by the nature out West, that kind of direct sense of being in it, as if I was walking through the words, as if through them I might touch the nature somehow

Also coming to see in the process of writing the poem in such a setting as this one that the instigation behind the poems was primarily experiential, i.e. I-centered, however much I would have preferred reflexively this not to have been the case, in such a setting as this one, coming as we did from Buffalo, New York. Yet realizing at the same time in such a setting as this one that at a certain point I've just got to be where I am, living with the words at hand, living, place to place, with them, not in them

In thinking these things, over and over again and again, I came as if suddenly to the realization, as if I had magically made some kind of leap, bypassing the necessary claims, grounds & warrants, that I had solved our problem, that the way to write the nature was through the language of catastrophe, what Paul Virilio calls the *accident*. He calls it a catastrophe too. A catastrophe materialized, or *metastasized*, in Buffalo but not as evident out West, due to the beauty, everywhere abounding. That if I must write these descriptive scenes/screens because of the power of these descriptive scenes/screens on the body and the mind's eye, and because of this desire to write, which is a desire for action, I must at the same time come to terms in the writing of these descriptive scenes/screens with the language of catastrophe, this particular one, right here right now, and that I could do so, first by collecting these catastrophic words, whenever I came across them, wherever we were, folding them in my notebook, the very same, skinny ($2'' \times 8\frac{1}{2}''$) notebook in which I drew these descriptive scenes, and that I could do so then by planting them, these damaged words, in the nature scenes, the scenes placed in these poems, in my skinny sky-blue notebook, planting them, in effect, these damaged words, in the park, in the woods, among the words found and heard there, as we walked in the woods among the words

Nature walks, steps
through signage

into the garden
of pleasure-

seeking trees
like firs pines and such

the moss-coated picnic tables
bright as blue velvet

makes looking feel
touched

X

wow that
trunk is huge

no, no wow
that or huge

X

A V

as in
view

through which
the   mountain

peaks
            pattern

X

  the path is slippery
i nearly slipped

X

in a fenced fog
through which

rendition

winds
   n binds

x-
    tra
      ordin
            arily

who knows
      who knew

X

this bed
of mixed

needles
embedded

in the creek
beneath

my clutch

X

walking through the letters

i found a # of alien words

some of which sounded

awfully familiar

X

that 4 in the forest
was for real a four

now too letters r
branching out

■

words go through
walls in through

people as
roving cameras

i'm like drifting
awake

■

between lines
the guard's rail

a long ways off
from the phos-

phorescent
hive

rapids rapidly
frothing

X

famously fresh
the vapor tumbles

organically over
insoluble treads

a decisive
inaction dis-

mounts

X

drawdown into
babbling rivulets

bubbles wobbling
for liberal light

▣

this notebook
w/ its narrow
  margins
around which
  the world
    press
     es
     in

▣

Sale (after Magritte)

this 4
is not

Shades don't function
in the forest the flash

of white between trees
the bars of the trees

such as firs pines
and such flum-

mox   the view

X

the path strolls through
the obstacle course

comes to a dead end
tires in trees things

here in the off season
literally not figuratively

out of reach ends
in a circle a cul-de-

sac to climb something
to do and so forth

X

a car shakes into action
and with its passing other

human sounds swirl
through trunks and trees

etc firs pines etc
as we read

X

a baby & kid [w/ mother]
skipping school

or is the forest their home
schooling

for the day
these their

disciplinary halls
so straight so tall

they school the eyes
flight-wise

X

y notes
    the y-

shaped tree,
the roaring

over
    heads

X

i don't hug
it
but run my hands
across along
it

Summer blue winter skies
and we're sealed, sick, inside

it's like i'm working

X

bands of yellow root
through the bars

of the forest wall
across the street

lighting up azaleas
and rhododendrons

and white fawn lilies
their "lance-shaped

oblong basal paired
leaves"

X

the fan's blades
singing in their cage

make themselves
k nown

X

put the enrollment form
with the check attached
        by paper clip
on the table by
the door
way

There is
the danger
of falling
trees etcetera
of poison
oak, and
rattlesnake

why this
urge to
take this
there to
replace
place

did some
body
do that

whose letters
line trees
or ferns or
webs or bird
song roughing
up a bush

is that disaster
on the lip of your
 hoot
        'n' holler

no stopping
the joggers
return to their
jobbers

please do
trespass
    adjacent
private bound
      ary

beneath
  zombie
      &
  butterfly
  co-
      mingle

pinched air
  bearing down
on this
  modulating
      pen

poe beside
the mud
dry interior
of root
system
breakdown

does the cat know
i'm playing this
twice in a row

surprisingly shallow
for such dizzy heights

as chance might
spell it

a new day dawns
for ponderosa

at the sound of
the rip

i can see it

your clearing
carved out
in blue

these trees
you know
they're so
lazy—
they just
stand there

Winter's defoliation
brings the neighbor

hood
to
mind

"Park Boundary"

on blue
posts

☒

orange flags
looped around
dangling branches

do not
denote

a heightened
security
alert

ridge is gone
and so too

the drill

X

poles in place
of sticks
click

w/ straps—

equipment

New York School

the snap

crackle pop of tires
on property

a single prop gurgling
even through   the
thickest of the thicket

laced in my *continuums'*
destining tread

that function freely in this
full-spectrum dominance
holding their course

incentive regulators
          a-warbling a-
cross the high windows

a red tail

and, on rings
of a felled fir, fungi too
red as black
          budget—

X

for Becky

figuring if
i run into a bear

i'll hand it my
billfold

but i left it in the
glovebox

drats!

X

he says in *the rings
of saturn* says he

*it seems a miracle
that we should last*

*so much as a single
day* — i too

hear voices & appeal
to a higher matter

this
spinning pulse

of the bossa
        nova
    disc

courtesy of
six degrees

for instance

there is no antidote,
he writes, writes he

& now me, all rights
reserved, except
for brief passages

it's moving
  page
        to page

brushing through
            the zoning
    the jack-

hammering inscription
of *melanerpes formicivorus*

as jonathan, you, my
friend, might say

X

grass tufting
next to
    a bouldering

large or smaller
it recruits them

aller

X

if i place them
here

i will, re
member
them

A shaft, with light, batteries across
morning's webs, like a-sparkling

teeth in a toothpaste ad
singeing the wires—birds

as such like so much techno
squonking *election*. chilled & boned,

i move with the moving,
here inside, the night

time's shadows lingering, at the nape
of the neck, hairs alight

as it goes. facing them down,
they go right back to work,

spinning, stitching,
wending, blending. look up

from this pad,
destabilized below

the breathing giants, careening
pioneer/deadly cargo. this what

looks to be
a maple branch is so long, stretching out

yards from its base, so far, that is, from
its trunk, it would seem, you would think,

still as it is stretching, to collapse
of its own horizontal positioning

or position-taking, a tree dreaming
of rhizomes or dreaming *in*

rhizome as if it were a language.
i bend and duck i hop over i place

my hand on the fallen, a log, straddle it my legs
around its faint familiarity, seemingly one

at a time up and over scraping across it
the bark worn smooth by others—hands

my hands these legs and the tree flesh
on dying flesh as it goes. weave

as the trail weaves, with paper in tow
parallels paralleling

the ups
& downs, white flying over

greens and browns, a pencil spinning
would-be silk-like

letters. the barbs of a long-rusted fence
gobbled up by what looks to be

an oak, swallowed like so many
hooks in the belly, like that

mechanical shark in *jaws*. a fern
stretches through the dreamy scene

to touch a startled hand, awakened
by some fellow in the yard below,

embedded in his habitus, who
looks past the forest & the trees

to his morning list. through the
skylight, the sun, angled against

the wall, performs
a triangulated shadow-play.

does he peruse the balcony?
has he read his jean genet? i move

on up into the palm of what i gather
are oaks, whose three fingers,

if we are to follow this trope, stretch
high above into the rocketing sky, as if

in the eyes' movement the trees
themselves move, mapping their history

from sapling to full-grown towering
redwood inferno, if you will, a new

sublime for the books. mosquitoes swoop
down from the above, trolling

for blood, a noisy feasting amplified
suddenly here in the ear. i move on

with the moving, through manhattan
-like towers, the scrapers, so tall at first,

shrinking in time, such that
you look up one day and feel concretely

the intimacy. on the map, this place
reads as a park, yet i seem

to have lost the trail and find my
self in blazing need now

of a machete, weed-whacker, predator,
what have you. ok, i've found the path again,

having taken the wrong fork, which, *natürlich*,
led me to these brambles, blackberry bushes

i believe. a line of blood etched above
one ankle pleases me. to no end. now

that i've found the path
again and again, i don't know

which way is up or what or where
this path is leading me.

up up up up, four ups
instead of three, to be precise, then

turn around and down
back thru 2 more downs, the

blood thumping through plaqued
arteries a-wiggling

like a worm on the back of so
many hands. here, under cover, alone

again (naturally), the humans
everywhere about me, up and down

all around inside out.
a salty chill murmurs

across the skin. papering along
through bands of adamsic light

parks next to a hovering
bee. this page has turned

into a butterfly
net. thinking humming

bird, of which many a species
here, in oregon, i am told.

pseudotsuga menziesii
lends a hand and I take

its so many words, steering me
back down again, past this then that

cognitive marker, this one possibly four
centuries wide arms extended. wow, said i as i

crossed it before, the dance of its spiraling limbs
way up high up there, see, shadowing me,

every step of the way, in a word, so much so
that i find now once again the letters' kiss

planted on my lips: "w" "o" "w," they
say. like a factory horn, a distant rooster

drives me down through a
series of wrong turns that empty

into a gravelly clearing of parked cars
and, beyond that, strapping an end to it,

the hot finality of willamette ave.
walking its asphalt back up the hill

toward the saturn, inside of which sits
the rings of saturn, past an elaborate

if apparently impressive automated
gate, with a box for strangers

to bark to, like, say, the pizza man, and a key
pad for those with the code, an estate

far out of sight, tucked away down
the long and winding road, an avenue

of its own, boasting its very own name
all to itself down there. then, finally, back

up one final hill to the south parking lot,
busy with like-minded vehicles,

and, end
of story,

the signage:
Park Closed

11PM – 6AM
ORD. 4.680

After Rilke

but my head said
my mind to its

private i is

an animal
synecdochic-

ally
speaking

yeah, right

🅇

the disappeared
reappear as fog

sunset downed by
trees of mystery

🅇

is there a signal
here or are we

out on
      the range

X

each peeved
at the very

sight
of park

the jolt
of the other

suddenly
on top

X

thin blue lines
rounds of ribbons

this one w/ pink
& black stripes

X

dapplings
dabbling

the doppler's
foreplay

X

bird
      sings

  or is that

        cherry

X

yr like really
at every turn
bugging me

X

blocks down &
bird's still
heard

☒

ferny fingers
fondling

a calf
a fawn

a doe's
deer

tho none's
here

presciently

☒

a conference call
or say a
        seminar

on thoreau say
fit as a meter

runnin
dwn

☒

the blast of the bell

in the beaker
says it all—

cherry

By Zuk, it <u>is</u>
a matter
of part

Ich!

At first I thought they
were swallow-
tails
but then realized they
        swallows

I take the shadows
off fold them
in   pocket
next to mechanical
                    pencil

I see they still
haven't cut them
down cleared them
out

I'm at the border
of a virtual
correction

Gone or
goners

Like this here particular native habitat:
                                        !

Why, uh, *are some of these*, uh, *trees*, uh,
painted? [cut paste move]

This morning
out my   shield

a high white line
[it's a contrail]

sharp, or *sharply defined,*
against *deep blue*, plunged

like a dagger
or *as a dagger*

into the doughy [snows]
head of Spencer

Butte, or *the round bust*
of Cézanne's Mont Sainte-V—

And just as I arrived,
a turkey buzzard, like
some kind of crazy omen,
flew its sexy bald head
straight into the forest wall

I was wondering why materiality
is still reduced to letters
& their words & their
entanglements, or

blackberry bushes

Why not the materiality
of their <u>vision</u>—

When I'm about
I write about

I find
I recollect, or *reconnect*

Going to the top?
  Oh, you know, I don't
 know

Web-light zinging
   past like

   LSD—*zing!*

Flashes of zong—
   some
 inspired
    or *gone!*

A car pulls into
the lot below
I hear it
turn off—that's life
life's lot, *over there*

Better space out

Does one
    begin to enjoy
        the manure
            in places like
                Nebraska?

Flower still closed at noon
sleeping off night—I can relate
or is it dead?

Must be these
        doomed
        blue
        ones
are held fast by the
        current
        budget
        impasse

If it weren't for us
we wouldn't have to
chop
        you down

This chip-
munk
appropriates
            the trail or
            my way
then dips down
under

That rattle
of construction
rhymes w/ yonder
        homes me in
        on a dime

And now we've come
full circle: ignition
never fails

These pink
buttercups—
can they
be pink

This red
clover—
can it
be red

Shelldwellers

"It was as if they were in a cage whose door was wide open, without their being able to escape. Nothing outside the cage had any importance, because nothing else existed any more. They stayed in the cage, estranged from everything except the cage, without even a flicker of desire for anything outside the bars."

—Raoul Vaneigem, *The Revolution of Everyday Life*

Is it enough simply to manage words? I ask. Anyone at all might touch them
If only for the words. Words are anywhere but here they remain relatively
Concrete, or *capable of sitting still*. You can put your happy finger on &/or in
(Not *w/in*) them and feel them wiggling with content. Stability stands, or

I prefer it seated. Starkly at odds, an odd ball, a strange "s." Furthermore, due to
Budgetary constraints, description has been capped. Disillusionment is forthwith
Guaranteed for those banking on code. Get over it. *I'm sticking to the backdrop,*
And can't pull free, yet I assert my positive feelings. What's there to add to this clear-

Cut, anyhow & all that besides. The trees up the street, some marked for
Clearance, have their own communicative action committee, or *CAC*. The light
Has been copyrighted and belongs to the highest bidder. Those below will grow

Stunted or adapt accordingly. Some thrive on the ground, produce deep cover.
Some crawl the walls, spiraling up toward the sun, on distended wings, where they
Wilt from exposure, or *intoxication*. Twinkies. Plop, or *gang bang*

How long before flex turns reflexive? The reporter used the word
At the press con, or *conference*, and our supercilious service rep went
Huh? Reflect-*ive*, replied the intrepid reporter, with belatedly evident
Contempt. Gotta work on that! We, my townspeople +

The meadow things   Perhaps I should lie about something.
Or maybe I just need the needle exchanged. The condensery works
Given you don't excise the indis-
Pensable. Step inside my ski boots. Preapproval ≤ preapproval.

Or *step into my oven.* Often I have this sense I am doing something
Wrong, I am about to get in trouble, someone's gonna catch me.
Or *wrong!* I ordered myself not to describe things, or *go emotional.*

I'm like anyone in my vehicle. Sometimes it gives me a feeling
I'm doing something. I'll be driving in car driving along, you know,
And suddenly realize I'm doing something

Boredom at Three, or *Gang Green in the Orange Zone*. Even the cells feel
Cellular, or *cushy*. Blame it on the infrastructure, or *blame it on pale Ramon*.
Legs shot from sitting day on day in desk. Desk = shell. Sure, that was
A year ago or so, or *have cell phones*, but encounters can't last, word has it.

Wandering takes you know where, this inflaming of the things, or *dwelling*
On path. Catch "worm dirt" on tickertape, or *acting as if we need only wait it*
Out. You wish. Your dish. Okay already I'll go to the meeting. Just don't ask
Me to go on record, or *host it* or *take notes*. Doctor says "probe" & the patients

Duck & cover, hunkering down yet "mobile on the spot," or *who needs to*
Walk? Missions fly south. Nothing to disillusionment, for they "have forfeited
A general presumption of innocence," or *up to my neck in pills*. Baudelaire says

It's like the gravest sin. But he wrote "ennui." We don't do that in the States.
Boredom never breaks the surface here, it's *all* surface, as in surface-to-air, or
Telematics. "A remarkable indifference" (Heidegger 88), world's hole, in one

Remind me again to live, meaning whatever. Why must life
Always come with these cabalistic frame structures? A cat forms
An interior. Why? I spent, the afternoon searching for that cat
Poem by Williams and got stuck inside *Spring and All* and all that.

Landscape: Alice Notley's "breakthrough book *Waltzing Matilda*"
Dips into "John Berger's *And Our Faces, My Heart, Brief as Photos*"
And the dewy dells of "enthymeme," pencil on white multipurpose paper.
Take a shot. Tear it up. This morning's brief, by noon's done. You can

Work them over all you want, but invention's spent; it's all
Management now. A calico simmers diagonally across the yard
And all that. Like a pair of pinking shears, for instance,

Swerving through velvet. The moss looks like it. Lichen
Edge the alders. The apple tree needs, pruning and so
Does. Especially I appreciate the fig alongside ours. Sun out

Line this room with cork and perhaps something will grow. A lineation
To unfold harmolodically. The floor gives way with a snap of two fingers
A hand dangling across its line. They are gathered around him
Like a commissioned painting. You can erase it later

Should the litigation arise. There's a memory hole for every occasion.
Is the Butte gendered female? I've never thought of her that way.
That she's a park means everything to me. I drive into it, tires crackling
Over, in this case, needles, every time, the pop of the parking lot's gravel.

Then I walk and then I feel the affectation. This place is like a cathedral
In that the trail produces quantum entanglement; it's all spooky action.
Birds chirping like an organ, man, and so forth. You'll have to throw in

Occasional hybrids, copters overhead, the pump of a podcast below, not
Unlike Cézanne's *Mont Sainte-V*. Check it out at www.planeteugene.com/
spencerbutte.htm & www.ibiblio.org/wm/paint/auth/cezanne/st-victoire

When hasn't it been a crisis? Me, I'm still in my pajamas. It's these states,
Or colonies, we're in, the brackets always shifting, yet stately still; is it real
Then, or is it just you and your silly putty? Why ask? These words, as placed
In this place, are flat from the start; the form fails, a priori. We like it

Like that, okay, or *make do*. By the way, per the severe: You're trying too hard.
Just let loose, breathe, please, as your grittin's gettin' to me, or *gathering gloom*.
Ah, our favorite theme, it would seem from the word count. It's easy:
Just click on the tools bar. Currently, we're five over the limit. Is that

The gimp you've got on your leash? A forest of gumps, who can't see the bunk
For the fleas. Get out the collar. Plowed under, this clear-cut feeling, by some
Kind of straight talkin' express governating 'cross the state; a full-court press.

Leaves you with a rash you can't help but scratch, or *Have we an ointment for you.*
That frown captioned on your face is sponsored by your can-do smile, on call
Seven twenty-four; useful, if not efficient; "arf" feels right, if unfair, for now

for Mark

Snow is worth noting. How it snows, not what. Sideways precisely there
Straightly down here. Humans can relate, if they adhere to certain distinct
Ways of carrying on; the golden rule, according to *Talk of the Nation*
Just this Wednesday. Cars and hills or *pills* don't mix well w/ ice; flat's

Fine, what's boring's safe, or *Safe*. With the infrastructure to handle, negotiate
The curves & *tight spots*. Yellowing moss against the green made the snow
Sickly w/ weirdly light, early this morning, or was it yesterday. The snow
Made the yard an oozing wound: moss-pus. A raccoon is worth the inkling,

Come sniffing around, of lately. Like the deer *hanging* several months back,
Scratched down, point blankly. Tony, that is. Then mid-ten, came the un-tame
Turkeys, crossing residential yards, plots. Worthy of note, all around, but not

Necessarily worth the cost of paper. A poem rarely is. For if the paper's
Of note, it's bound to be a tax & spender. A healthy, sustainable lounge-like
Loafer, on the other hand, is, while dumb, funner, indeed, to be

I should title it "Sonnets in Search of a Job." As "job" is embedded in
The punch line, or *paratexas*. Dostoyevsky wrote those novels for cash,
You know, to pay off his gambling debts, or *debits*. Many poets write
With a job in mind but few write it inside their poems. To write

Of it here, inside a sonnet, which stands for purity, is scandalous,
Hopefully, or *Scandinavian*. A sonnet is a way of structuring attention.
Write one today and you have the weight of lyric poetry on your back,
A metronome hamming it home like some Kenny G wannabe. I try

To stay in sync, but I just can't fell the timber. It's like N trying to sleep
Last night, wailing her inner beast deep into the moonlit night, or
Midnight Madness. Of course, not really "wailing." I can't *do* IT. Schedule a life

Around pleasure. Clichés work too. Do what you want and don't take advice.
Time's not as short as they say and death is a continuous yawn, or *yarn*. Don't
Waste your time thinking it's gonna teach you anything

I always mean to do more. Not chores but substantial stuff.
Fill it out if you wish. It's not as if it's *my* language, my language
Alone. You can do it if you believe it and if you don't believe
There's plenty left undone. But there's more to life than

Living. Some of this comes from grading papers and running into
Sentences that are *out there*. Words like *definitely* are out there.
This is defiantly in the American grain. "'I'm a poet, I'm emo
Tional, I'm writing about my feelings'" (Ch.B.). "You hurt

My feelings" (children expressing). *Say it.* Words sit in watch,
Like this and that. Harassed simultaneously by three discrete forms
Of nag factor. Word's *out there*: We Americans, by which I mean

US, we're dupes. Why does it always come back as a wake-up
Call? The clock's set on snooze, doofus. Periodic alarms
Make dreams come alive. There are eight in all

How do you stop a word from popping up like a cookie? You
Start out with *invention* and end up on *convention*, which is a lower
Score. What's a song without a melody? you ask. A song that makes
Melody of the cracks. *Got that?* It's like you're nowhere more present

Precisely as you're shifting. Jobs should stay put, though. I want one
That's tedious but short. A job I can dream on, so I can get back to
Work. This scenery stinks of economics. Dish out a few particulars and
You've got a full meal (the kind that makes you famished in a short hour), or

Can I go now? You want extra sauce just so it tastes like anything, or
A debriefing system. Here's a list and a pencil for marking off, a residual form
Of labor, shoveled under like so much, if I may, raw sewage. Brings us back

To the same spot of time, or *back to the future.* Is the brain a taser? Can
Spring cleaning cleanse? Coffee and the news do not make a mise-
En-scène. What *is* found there? Hit the space bar to get a clue

Your blowback needs a hanky. The cursor flies high like a doomed
Duck. What's a sin? she asks. Living in a rain forest makes the onto
Logical tactile. What am I, a brochure? Yes is the answer, love is the
Blooper. We all have our maps to perform. Deer walk upon our prop

Erty. Golly, far out, shut up. Get real inside the grain. It's hard to know
What to keep, or *it's hard to know what you're looking at when friends
Morph into lizards.* Why can't you say it the way you means? Yes well
He works there so he looks at it different. But then we're all peacekeepers,

Each in our own carnivalistic fashion. Just blink several times in a row
Fast. You smell like *TV Guide.* This disjunctive death tax is not I say
Is not symptomatic of our remote control culture but rather simply

A career move. A sin, Binky, is when you do something
You don't believe in repetitively, w/ relish.
Hold the mustard gas, I got the president on the line

It's not me capitalizing the situation here. Just as green and red
Lines appear phantasmagorically below key words, so too
Capitals from the start. I could fight it, but now I'm locked down
In the zone, I'm squandering all my leads, or *troop levels*.

I've lost the compass but gained a meter. It's like when you're
Downsized and you're struggling to think positive act big and so
You tell yourself it's the start of something new, that it's life's way
Of telling you what to do. Nomads prefer escapism. But there's no

Walking away from this prison house of langpo. Whose new
Sentence is this and what's it doing inside my sonnet? Is this torque talk
Akin to my Hemi? And is that Chevy or Bjork? Benchmarks

Are for the benched. Go low inside. Drive and dish, bust
A zone. Open looks are Keystone Cops. There's a hand in the picture
Directing things but everyone's smiling individuated ways

Perhaps first thought worked best because it produced (we're running
Out of time or, *down time*, after all) more poems, a greater body and range
Held together by their absence of correction. Err is their fare, their
Force, what keeps them alive, if we agree with Bernhard that correction's

Finally suicide. If perfection's so rare, why do we value it so? I mean,
You'd think we'd want something we could experience on a more
Daily ongoing basis. Like boredom. And in any case perfection today
Is affection for the grand afflictions, no? The *Pierre*s, of this world.

Things change, enough to return, true. But if it returns is it change or
Chomsky? He's looking old, of late. Seen him on C-SPAN, where else,
Methodically excoriating a cynic: things are for the better

Even as they're getting worse. Extinction lingers in these lines. Nibbles
Away at the letters; they're fraying, it would seem, even as they appear intact.
As when cleansed, the fabric naturally thins—*it's trickle-down time, baby*

The aim is to drift, mainly on the plane, or *on plateau*. It's hard,
Though, I know I know, going sideways when you've been making
Progress all your life, or *when you're on the escalator, the escalator*
Of successive regime change. But a poem requires a steady wand.

The belt buckle clanking in the dryer is worth a thousand points
Of blight. The buzzer's labor. A fan distributes the wealth,
Measured in motes, or *dust motes*. A swirling cloud of dervish
Calls for a clean in out skirmish of choice; just, or not

Do it. Builds a memory of summer, when, you know, the light
Draws closure upon the immanent. Rilke's thing's a piece
Of past. So is Trakl a rash? *"A"'s* still on my A list. I travel

Through books instead of reading them. You'll find their vapor
Trails scattered across the mortgage. Sirens are barreling down
The hall to be re-alphabetized by the order of things

I went / To word / Today. Or one of the parts I like most is you can use it
Is you can use it and ignore it at the same time. In any case, why "utmost"
And why "meaning" and why "charged"? Why "to" "the" "with" "language"?
Ours is worst than yours though yours surely was *the worstest*. And long, not

Short. We've turned a new leaf and it's flaking already. I feel botched, frankly,
An old cyborg squeaky in the knee. The snows of Kilimanjaro are no more
No more. Trickles down to a contest in Key West, some kind of disneyfied
Kentucky fried key largo fandango. Is a sonnet a sin? There are statements

And there are commandos, but there are also quatrains without facemasks.
Castration of the man in *Rome* flows into *Iran Build-Up*. Advertising is the glue
To my wet dreams, but this *bürgermeister* is out of control, or *show me the way*.

Teach me something in delightful groans, or *with dissonant bush*.
Scratch me some fancy lyric on your Aeolian turntable,
"I'll fuck anything that moves," or *what kind of "degree"*

My beautiful mind likes its cake, sure, but a hearty loaf
From the local boutique's grand, if you can. We like ours
With tapenade, an olive spread from Provence, that's
France, which is best served on crostini.

Oh yes, believe you me, there's nature all around us as we move.
Peel back any can of words. 'Twas more lyrical in Buffalo, with its
Grain elevators rising atop the detoxed swamp, expired fish
Corpsing up the shoreline. Here in Oregon, it's strained, tinny,

Never mind the clear-cutters' *craft*. They bring us down to rocky
Earth. How is it this pastoral-like valley scene gets linked to
Libido? Can't a guy wax poetic on the streets for some change

W/o getting booted to the Bronx? This dirty cloud is fogging my
Solar anus. We don't do body counts. Bring on the rain.
Words serve as excellent cover. Words like "Heck"

What do I do with the day? There's no way I'm going to take stock.
What, do I look like a jock? I spend my time drawing up character sketches
Of the neighbors & sic them on each other. Plath going nuts
Comes to mind, or some such fictional get-up. Though, it's not like

I'm married to no Mr. Hughes. Though she'll probably trash mine
Too, but good thing. I mean, I'd want that. Just today for example
I checked out some old stuff and, yikes, it was bad. Why do I stick with
This business? I don't know about you, but don't you sometimes wonder

How you ever ended up in this *situation*, as W would say? I can't get him out
My head; I must kind of like love him or something; it's like I'm a *shrubaphobe*
As dear deceased Molly would say. Things are really that bad, OK.

So let's all stop working so much and relax to save the planet.
Do these Washington politicians really have lemonade parties?
Is that some kind of sick joke, Alicia Keys? Bob, help me out here

We step outside the box for a smoke + talk. We are the healthiest
As we get all the breaks. It's a smokers' polis; the rest of us
Are just passing through, in pods. Whereas in the prior series a semi-
Colon is a momentous occasion, here it's just part of the corporate

Bundle, spare parts from our inner Stasi. Squatting on the rocks, they
Look up from the laundry at a parcel of neo-colonials on horseback,
Bright eyes on an après-school spin. Shy, perhaps blushing, an inner voice
Peeps out its shell, where it dwells for a spell, only to crawl back

Into its stock and trade. Hence this dumping out to see what grammar's
In place. This is the true lesson of Vietnam. Syndromes fade fast
With every rinse cycle. Where two, udders distended, suddenly as one

Stood, plus signing statements, the multitude groped under the gun
Of its polyverse, duking it out, that's a boxing term, in the halls
By watercooler meme. This event produced a crinkle in the voltage

I'm depressed, polls show. My shoulders slouch on this shrinking world,
Or *shrink-wrapped world*. Holding it in, the bubble, as they squabble over
Top-ten moments. Who cares is all I got. It's not shrinking, it's *alive!*
And, well, taking over. I look forward to teleporting out of hot spots.

I think, you protest, or you protest too much, or not enough, what is it?
I figure if I write enough long enough my absent center will kind of like
Leap unto its own. This is definitely autumn air flapping through the
Torn screen. Torn because I walked into it the other day, now it's like

A curtain keeping out some of the bugs but not all. Spiders make a home
Of our house but that's life if you expect to live in this neck of the hegemony.
It means walking through webs all the time and settling with the verisimilitude

Of lack of career *give-o-fuck*. I think my decision or rather tendency
Decision is too decisive to put it off must come in part, in part always of
Course, from various symptoms attacking my internal organs somewhere

This leisure, passed leisurely with loving care, produces
A tumor in the breadwinner's brain. For a house is a wreck
Without its maid, which in Aristotle's time was the woman
Of the house, plus her slaves. Off the clock, leisure slides in

Lackadaisically, and is taken in readily, with shining ease. I neglect
The dishes, respectfully, as the washer's sound irritates the calm
Crucial for truly genuine, leisurely activity. Warm weather, after so many
A damp February May day, brings out the labor in the hood. Men

Are digging up the yard, across the street. Flooding in the basement.
There's a river underneath, running wild, I'm told. Down the way
The guy's ripping out his bushes on his new lot. He's tearing down

His ol' wooden fence & mending it with chain link, which has altered
My perception. *Ostranenie*'s rare in these parts so I take it in link by link.
Oregon oaks in front, all gangly and unseemly, remain intact, so far

Words need breaks too. But don't expect to get anywhere with it except hired
At best. Which is a step backwards in as much as time has now been snatched
From you and you only have so much time. But you need the cash. Not lots
For gosh sakes, just enough for your theory of everything. I've punched in

And look what it's gotten me, or *a bruised scalp*. Poetry puts the job in its place,
I like to think. Like laminate floors, or the 100% synthetic leather dining chairs,
Fresh from the box, that ran close to a grand in cost. Not that the life squeezed
Into writing is yours, even when it's seemingly all about you you use. Still, it's

Easy for us to get confused and start taking it personal. When she was born, I
Leapt ahead two decades and found myself walking in the same sneakers but
Close to the edge. It was like it was always-already over-already, happily. Foucault

Would say this sort of quasi-confession weakens your positioning, even if *faux*, as
It's now on record, dummy. But: is a poem a record? Fact or fiction? Time
Is money & poets are supposed to be poor. And Foucault, didn't he drive a Jaguar

I see nothing but song upon song, one negating the other, like some kind
Of Hegelian free fall, backward-somersaulting up the butt-hole of history.
Happiness slithers behind its velvet curtain, all smiles like it's a dirty in-
House joke, or *Huh?! What?!* That's why I go all nasty, whether in cubicle

Or at counter, or *behind the wheel*; it's all me all the time, swerving here,
Lurching there, screeching and singing and calling out. This living business,
Or *busyness*, gives off the feeling of replay: whose lines are these coiling off
The prompter, whose greasy elbow leaning on my pleasure key? It's not like

I'm not like a total original, you know, a bonafide, one-of-a-kind ghetto
Superstar, or *an upside-down snowflake in the Baselitz mode*. As a symptom, I'm
Fighting back warning signs like I'm stuck inside a Jane Fonda cliché.

Fondue, anyone? Or say it's a fishing trip with *the guys*, all of us pre-
Twilights, popping Flomax as we reel in the trophies. Free, at last, to pee,
As frequently as may be, for the sheer, sweet sensation of its splashy reverie

Go go—*go*, into the dewy dawn, like a baby slip-sliding through the rubber
Gloves of a part-timer. For I'm always-already a goner, squirting across
My own juicy excess in the galaxy of my manstink, or *the waxy way of mine own*
Pet newt. It feels right to own a nipple. Amphibian, retard. As a kid, I was into

Salamanders, you know. They're not lizards, but lizard-like, except for their move
Ment, which is slower, more deliberate. And some other particulars like that. In
Here, it's a matter of doing time, and so what's said is as good as anything as
Long as it lasts; though, occasionally, we *do* get complaints of abused substance.

Life is long / if you give it away. True, dude! And good quote! Generally speaking,
You don't want to quote something mundane, that you could easily have said your
Self. The Byrne above is good quote 'cause paraphrasing it would lose the magic

Of its way it's put. If you sell out and do as you're told, life is like unbearably long.
But if you follow your manstink and stay true to your innards, then life's short
As hell. It's like life's likely to creep up and kill your ass for being so authentic

Wonderful Chords

"It doesn't have to be boring, predictable pop; pop can be like this, the drums can sit back, the percussion can be textile, the horns can grow and swell, the strings can be sweet as jasmine; in other words, don't be embarrassed; enjoy the sense of wonder that chords can bring."

—Sean O'Hagan

Time to re-tire, think
deserted coves

The protected valleys
and alluvial flats

A most sensual haven
for those no longer

Looking

If only everything in life
were broadly funnel shaped

A low, tufted, densely
yellowish disk with leafy rays

With reds, pinks, and cream-
colored confidence

I was fondling a tangerine,
sampling voices from afar

Yet close at hand, while those
nearby

Were strumming
thick-textured, piquant flavors

Prickly as the sweet
hereafter

I really see now

What a delightful place
can do

With roundish heads
and the soft spot

Enjoy
a pair of clear eyes

Dropped
in a green glen

Preying
on the marbled murrelet

In the hollers of junk dna
pleasing people

The planet over
confident

Of what a smile can
make

Of moral
                hazards

With right service and prime price,
where age-old

Fish cages, wavy and toothed,
forever flourish

Kid-tested, mother-approved,
greenish-white and bowl-shaped,

Deeply cleft, professional grade

We relaxed in hammock
the lighter way to cool off

Under a hairy plant
and you daydreamed

Of world events crowding your mind
like a Gerber baby

Distinctly veined—
suffering the amazing view

For we love to see you smile, bright
yellow flower head, ever-enfolding

In the leaf-like bract reached by
seaplane

Looking for
a picker-upper

The undeadness
of the Good

And bountiful
sand piper

Moving our tales
like we're lovin' it,

We're the empire
of now

Lividly rich
      and muzzled

The future's bright
you feel like a nut

A little dab'll do ya
such as tanoak

Or Pacific
      madrone

A smooth tenderness
a carpet of filmy strings

Weightless and humming
in the lush foam

With lime green,
tremolo, and a mini bar

Pyramids of red, green and
gold

The parping trumpets
of Jack's moonbeam

Sunset cruises into green
percussive soul twangs

And crisp know-how,
the ultimate source for

Everyday needs

It's what's
for dinner

Snowy plover
and chinquapin

Pid e rick, or "Do Not Cite, Quote, or Distribute"

"Smell the sea, it's over the dunes, down
the ocean road."

— Sean O'Hagan, "Take My Hand"

These catastrophic words,
       these atmospheric burdens,
              folding them in my sky-blue notebook,
           planting them in the digital meadow flarf
                 like some kind of Johnny Seed-Saver
                               woika woika woika [2.2.1]

Some kind of action
           leans into the screen,
               a trick played on the pupils, real
                            as fictitious capital
          slapping the ozone about
              like some kind of furlough,
                 some kind of contract all tore up / spent,
     drippings from pre-1980 values,
          where thousands of stars once twinkled [2.2.2.7]

Dreamt up in aching sunshine
        by a frisky would-be harmonica
            surfing the waves of green imagination—
     this spadix-like every-figure
   dragging his burden across the ice drifts, bent
               to the task, ever ready
                 at hand
          witchety witchety witchety witchety [2.4.1.3]

Moderate rains sweep through
      with the soft permission of supple wonders
          serious relaxation in the swollen sun
              you can smell the sea rising
                  tsee tsee tsee tsee tsee [2.7.2]

Luxuriant pastiche, home to banana slugs
      and beach pea,
        "there will be
      a hissing and a curse,"
            tsiptsip tsee di di,
              tsiptsip tsee di
                di [2.4.1.1]

Kuk notes, set in motion
      by some lyrical brand,
        nothing too grand—
          takes my hand and runs it through the sand
      the whole thing is gently propulsive
           like the amazing blue-eyed eel [2.4.4]

Frahhhnnk, "I see thirst,"
      in canoe or kayak, loafing or consuming,
    "where half the population lives," grayish small
        externalities,
    pelicans, sea stars, carousing shrubs,
          creates better stream substrate [2.6.2.2]

Roughing them up
        with string section schmaltz
not a lifting or release but a swarming
        like a flurry of painted birds
                splashing about
        a snow white figurine [2.5.7]

White belly, rich chip, thin, sharp *pik*—
        lounge-ready, with all the native glee you please—
                bee please be, remain, ouch! *that stings*—
                        but we miss their continuous functioning—
                                shaark shaark shraak [2.7.7]

Summer's gone
        all cotton-candy grape-
                        like [Box 2.5]

Once abundant, now
                in imminent danger,
        fuzzy-headed and suicidal—lung-
                        damaged Gulf-
                                coast *piik sreep* [2.7.7]

Ice blotched axils in the great dying area,
        "a switched-on universe" w/ "no off-switch" (24/7) [2.6.2.2]

Articles can be
beautiful too
can conjunctions,
sun-dappled
with delirious signal verbs—[2.6.1]

A purple dreamer, sneezy chup, wispy
with vivid imagination
& the fluty *toop toop* [Box 2.5]

Huge boulders of pink individualized texture,
ideal gas lands, *wek wek wek wek wek wek* [2.7.8]

Brightly polished with tenderness and
unfussy warmth, wide blue history
listens in, world-whipped
by emerald budgets
and blackened sight, not to mention
surface temp *wek* [2.4.2]

Confidence is low, a key conical bill,
uncertainty is medium,
between liquid datasets, weedy fields,
a because clause of indecisive cloud banks
and poleward shift, supplies collapse,
a vast pool of seltzer, ice-free aspects
in the AR4, *krrok ook* [2.4.4]

Pid e rick, feeds on refuse, handouts,
                        in triple-thick canopies, frequents
                                    white wing bars, chisel-like,
                tree-clinging behavior, helps
        stabilize stream banks, answering each   other
            in limbic jumble of warbled note,
                pinkish flower, mist *medium*—
                            afterwards, slow rhythm
                                and multiple secrets, *ooo eeek* [2.2.1.1]

        Sweetly scented glaucous light,
                            ice-free by mid-century—

"those damn goal posts keep moving"

        "sidd says: 'There are many wonderful places
                            we will never see in the sun
                    and the breeze again'" [2.7.5]

            sidd says:
            "I weep
            for those
            to come
            who will
            never see
            that wonder"

                    Heads relaxing under thatched roof
                    in the dining area, 40% loss, irreversible
                    fifty-gigaton burp, sings from high perches

year round, *nyeeah*, outdoor shower, rising
1–3 meters, swinging horns, burble & blip &
bree dee dee [2.7.5]

*AIC says: "What am I misunderstanding? The IPCC Website has a button for Full Report,
but what I am downloading has on the bottom of each page: 'Do Not Cite, Quote, or Distribute'"*

Crucial strings swirl upward into wild kindness

Crystalline burdens caress paintbrush-like luxuriants

Fleshy pixiphones canter through elliptical havens of wah-inflected fruit meadows

Lush hills slap the ozone into splendid underwater flora

Fresh and cool furloughs spiral upwards into wispy and wondrous ice-drifts

Chipmunks, raccoons, rabbits brought to a gentle canter with the blue-eyed eel

Giant tortoises browsing the prairies for banana slugs and huckleberry surface *wek*

Harsh conditions clanging through a fabulous afternoon nap

Our names hissing in the back dunes where stars once twinkled

Heart-shaped facial discs crowned by prominent ear tufts

> *who cooks for*
> *you, who cooks*
> *for you allll* [2.3.3]

About the Publisher

Airlie Press is run by writers. A nonprofit publishing collective, the press is dedicated to producing beautiful and compelling books of poetry. Its mission is to offer writers working in its particular habitat a local, shared-work publishing alternative. Airlie Press is supported by book sales, subscription orders, and donations. All funds return to the press for the creation of new books of poetry.

Other Titles from Airlie Press

Donna Henderson *The Eddy Fence*
Jessica Lamb *Last Apples of Late Empires*
Anita Sullivan *Garden of Beasts*
Carter McKenzie *Out of Refusal*
Cecelia Hagen *Entering*
Chris Anderson *The Next Thing Always Belongs*
Stephanie Lenox *Congress of Strange People*
Annie Lighthart *Iron String*
Dawn Diez Willis *Still Life with Judas & Lightning*
Karen McPherson *Skein of Light*

X

Colophon

Titles and text are set in Arno, a modern serif font
based on typeface styles of the 15th and 16th centuries.
Named after the river that flows through the city of Florence,
Arno draws on the warmth and beauty of the
early humanist typefaces of the Italian Renaissance.

X